To my grandfather, John Westley Robinson, who was born into the institution of slavery in the mid-1800s. He persevered and became a farmer and a successful entrepreneur who loved poetry. He died a freeman at the age of ninety-nine. God bless you, John Westley Robinson.

PREFACE

Below the rim of heaven, we are all children of God, regardless of religious order, denomination, or faith. We strive desperately to come to grips with our mortal existence, restoring order to the infinite complexity of our lives. My poetry takes you to a higher level of understanding where emotion, not intellect, defines the uncertain relationship with our creator. It transcends all international, cultural, social, and eternal boundaries. My message is one of hope where there is despair, love where there is reluctance, and joy to soothe your heart.

DONNELL PERRYMAN

BELOW THE RIM OF HEAVEN

Library of Congress Control Number: 2013918586

ISBN: Softcover   978-1-4931-1498-6
       Hardcover   978-1-4931-1499-3
       EBook   978-1-4931-1500-6

Print information available on the last page.

Rev. date: 04/17/2017

To order additional copies of this book, contact:
Xlibris
1-888-795-4274
www.Xlibris.com
Orders@Xlibris.com

CONTENTS

My Knight in Shining Armour

Let me shield you inside my heart
When your fragile world has come apart
Let me shine light into your perilous dark
I'll illuminate your world; I pledge my heart
Let me be your greatest champion
I would gladly give my life for thee
I will slay all of your fiercest dragons
If you would just love and honor me
I have loved you, it seems, forever
Always, my esteem has been from afar
You are my beautiful, glorious princess
You captured my spirit; I surrendered my heart

Tale of Two Stars

I cast my heart with all of my might
Into a golden star with a jaded light
My heart was pure; the timing was right
I deflected this star from its orbital flight
So foolish to cast a heart into an empty night
Into a golden star that spurned its light
My fragile soul could not melt the ice
I bowed my head, crying through the night
My shattered heart fell from this sky
Into a vibrant star, into a soothing light
It composed my mind, eased the strain
It kissed my brow, removed the pain
Having cast my battered heart
Into this simply wondrous new star
I was blessed with the solace of love
A celestial jewel, I'd been longing for

My Life

We who are at the uncertain age of vulnerability
Our once-brilliant lights softly fade to somber gray

Sadly, once-potent minds begin to drift and wander
To a glorious time when precious dreams did not slip away

Where are those who vowed to love us unconditionally?
Where are those who promised to protect our hearth and home?

Placed in a home where there is a serious lack of compassion
Who are you to tell me that I can no longer live alone

There is a part of me that will never-ever surrender
A rebellious spirit inside of me seeks to right this ungodly wrong

Why cast me away, deliberately plowing my dignity under?
I have earned the right to make my life my own

Do you really believe I'm too old, too weak, and defenseless
I've retained the greatest defender the world has ever known

I know of one whose powerful presence gives me hope eternal
In his eyes, I am more precious than the rarest stone

Don't set me aside as if I don't understand your real intentions
Until you've walked my path, my true heart you'll never know

I have lived my life never compromising my true convictions
That being, God and only God would rule my soul

Little Mickey

No one knows when he went away
He was here one day; he quietly slipped away
Took it for granted that he would be here today
A baseball in hand, a beautiful smile upon his face
Many are deceived when the dark angel comes
Sword of life in hand, a precious name on his tongue
Please do not endeavor to mourn his unlikely fate
At this very moment, Mickey walks in amazing grace
I know we try to understand the things we cannot see
We repine a promising future never meant to be
We try to reopen doors that have no keys
We close our logical minds; we refuse to believe
Please try to understand-- little Mickey is in God's hand
He is part of an awesome and glorious master-plan
His heavenly father, the one who closed his little eyes
A body must be at rest before a beautiful soul can fly

The Devil and Westley Bones

Westley Bones, Westley Bones,
why does your weak soul keep on holding on?
Your daddy's a lush, your grandpa went nuts,
and your poor mama is probably stoned.
Your unfaithful wife left home, your money is gone
and your best friend was just hit by a bus
Your dog just died, and your horoscope lied
when it said you had suffered enough.
Your future looks grim and your prospects are slim;
the bank just foreclosed on your house.
My sympathies brother, they just arrested your mother,
and your psycho sister just strangled her spouse.
I guess you're down on your luck, times look tough
but your ole buddy Lucifer won't let you down.
Yo, Bones! Your car got jacked, mother-in-law is back
Your beloved parakeet was just eaten by a stray cat
So why look at me grinning through your teeth?
Your whole world is coming down around you, fool!
You are making me mad; I'll grab you, lad,
and gladly beat that Holy Ghost crap out of you
Look at me, Bones! Really, I should have known.
Did you place your faith on Jesus's throne? Damn!

Wonder

Frolicking through open meadows
splashing creeks with cold, wet toes
Possessing energy, which seems eternal
bright eyes and runny nose
Frogs hidden in your pockets
shooting marbles with flecks of gold
Fresh minds, which see into tomorrow
young minds, that can never grow old

To My Loving Brother

A shocking revelation, the news that you had died
So utterly stunned was I—I've really yet to cry
Neither tears nor sadness have marred my face
The banked fires in my soul fill an empty space
You gave me hope when my hope had expired
You fought a great fight; you never questioned why
A struggle so monumental, surely you'd beat the odds
Know that you're my hero; you inspired my broken heart
To win this battle of life is like climbing the steepest hill
It's never about how we died but a testament to how we lived
Dear brother, your life was special; it held a hidden key
It unlocks the door to heaven—it's meant to set us free
Love you, Daryl

The Invalid

Let my spirit soar in the breast of an eagle
let it explore the endless, gray sky
I shall challenge the ageless thermals
wings which dance where men dread to fly

Place your essence upon my wing tips
let us embark into the rising sun
A place of marvel, mystic wonders
a vast eternity where all life was born

My spirit graces the far realms of heaven
my useless legs will forever be asleep
If I cannot walk among men as an equal
God, let me soar beyond their reach

Rain

Splitter, splatter on your pane
Splitter, splatter the lovely rain
Splitter, splatter all over your house
Splitter, splatter the world throughout
Splitter , splatter on your beautiful face
Splitter, splatter on the whole human race
Splitter, splatter rain is God's grace

Soaring

Soaring ever so high in a sky so blue
where do flying objects generally land?
Young, fretful minds really don't have a clue
Will it descend in the awful neighbor's yard?
Worse yet, will it hit mom's brand-new car?
Fate, so unpredictable when objects travel so far
An errant ball hits a windowpane
a host of running and frightened kids
Only God knows who'll take the blame

Missing You

It was extremely cold today
my heart was warm in a special way
I made many plans today
thoughts of you would lead me astray
It felt like the same ole day
my mind was strong; my laughter, gay
I had great expectations today
but the vigor in my soul would not stay
Lady, I missed you today

My Brother

My brother is a selfish, rich man
his heart is ruled by greed
My brother is a lowly beggar man
stretching out his cup in need
My brother is the terminally ill man
a dying body racked with disease
My brother is a humble, poor man
praying profoundly on his knees
My brother could be a black man
he could even be Japanese
My brother lives in the realm of God
my brother is any man you see

Going Home

One day, you will look for me
but you won't find me here

One day, you will cry for me
but I will not see your tears

One day, you will search for me
but I'll be already gone

So please don't distress yourself
there is really nothing wrong

My heavenly father called to me
I didn't just leave—I went home

Grandpaw

Love me with your mind
while I can still read it in your face

Place your flowers in my hands
do not wait to place them on my grave

Love me for just this day
my fragile tomorrow might slip away

Let's walk hand in hand
let's go watch your children play

Come, cry softly upon my shoulders
let warm tears stream down upon my face

Such a waste of needless sorrow
who would dare to mourn my fate

For I go on to a brand-new world
I go on to a brighter day

Do You Believe

Do you believe what you really can't see?
You uproot a tree; explain the notion of free
Basking your head in the soothing rains
will a mind ever be devoid of pain?
You surround yourself in the latest fashion
now put on your most ardent compassion
Right and wrong are just two words in a song
millions of words explain what's already known
Bragging about your brand-new ride
can you really subdue your rebellious pride?
Drinking rotgut whiskey down on the corner
don't hide your head-- you have no honor
Putting on makeup to distort your face
unfortunately, you will never save grace
Do you really believe what your mind conceives?
Really!

A Man's Love

A man's love is not a timid love
expressed in a whimper, a sob, or cry
A man's love is a basic love
a simple nod, stern look, or quiet good-bye
A man's love is not a shallow love
you watch it swell in the depths of his eyes
A man's love is a tremendous love
he'll love you with his strength and might
A man's love is such a perfect love
a love you can treasure for life

He Who Loves the Rock

What must you see when you look at me
a rough countenance and stern look to my eyes

What must you believe when a young mind perceives
the timeworn furrows forged in my brow

I know what you see when you scrutinize me
an inner toughness I know I can't hide

As a father, I realize when you look into my eyes
you seek only the love I keep deep inside

The Woods

Deep in the farthest reaches of your mind,
there is a wooded glade where real love abides
Prepare to scramble below the brambles of degradation
and climb the steep and lonely slopes of real frustration
If you really want to find the exact location, be patient
this narrow pass is chock-full of sheer aggravation
You'll scamper over the festering pits of mindless bigotry
cross the awful swamp where pure hatred builds its lair
Keep going until you reach the hell-spawn desert of futility
turn left and cross this raging river of deep despair
Run fast, or you'll face an extremely, monstrous ego
please, don't look back or foolish pride will eat you alive
Once you've crossed the narrow bridge of true compassion
leaving all biased thoughts straggling, hopelessly far behind
Then and only then, will you find this splendid paradise
hidden in your mind

Farewell to Life

My body is quaking; my faith is shaking
God, the day is long—there's something wrong
The sun is colder, my disquieted mind gets bolder
A sky encased in a dome; a silence that's much too strong
Even my simple heart attempts to deceive me
Into its structured, sanctioned web it would weave me
Using the very essence of love, it dares to cleave me
Facts are still unknown—truth has not come home
My universe feels wrong; my tears flow freely on
Upon the harps of eternity; if God would conceive my song
The first precious line would read~~ our baby is gone

Butterfly Leaf

Let us fly into a cloud—it's the wonder I seek
Only solitude to be found among the highest peaks
Soaring, the only escape from any earthly claims
I'm one of the special ones with the broken wings
I feel free in the air; I would dare to be so bold
Only wind and sky will ever touch my troubled soul
To Cloe

Sky Children

Surviving, striving, dying in dark alleyways
processed in city morgues, buried in nameless graves
These are the realities which exist today
in this so-called land of the free and home of the brave
Homeless children without hope, without a face
society's blight, humanity's disgrace
Drugs, dope, sexual assaults
no mothers, no fathers, no protection from the law
Tears show fear, and cowards don't live
only the tough survive the awful, dreaded puberty years
They will avoid "the man" and run if they can
"take me to juvenile hall, bro, who gives a damn"
Sleeping, leeching, no more tears left to cry
eager to steal any fool's slice of the American pie
Dreaming, scheming, trying to get through another day
"my little brother got killed, I barely got away"
Crying, dirty, bathing only if it rains
hopeless eyes, tough bodies, small minds racked with pain
Walking curb gutters, begging on city streets
small bellies growling, out of trash cans they eat
Knife fights over garbage rights
small bodies found in the early morning light
Yet we close our eyes; we turn our heads
in our extravagance, we still dare to waste our bread
Young children walking in the night
troubled eyes downcast, feet ready to take flight
There was just one who looked into the sky
there was only one who believed that he could fly

Kindred Souls

Look at me, if you truly want to see
just look beyond the color of my skin
I look at you, and beneath you I see
the naked soul locked so deeply within
I am more than just another
I am more than just your brother
I'm without a single doubt
your fellow kindred soul
Our minds may disagree
social barriers too high to breach
But we must both strive
to walk the same road
In life, we share a common goal
that being to purge our inner souls
If not, then the key to heaven
God will never ever unfold
I look critically at you
and you look seriously at me
We are both shocked to see
we're from the same similar mode
On the street, as strangers we meet
a smile is just a start
Don't just look at me, look in me
and judge me from my heart

Hope

Here on the green fields of eternity,
lies that which was I; the earth my bed
rocks, the only monument of my passing
My body held firm to the earth
by the unshakable hand of death
my inescapable, silent companion
Time and reality is thoroughly shattered
flowing together towards a mystic sea
To die is to know what has gone before us
what is and what the afterlife will be
Reality, the first act of a two part drama
of life, death, and an alternate visionary
I'm alone yet not alone, I'm the soft breeze
I blow quietly among a sun-glossed meadow
love, hate, and fear are unknown to me
I am the crawling things in the earth
creeping through shadowy paths to feast
and in due course, to be feasted upon
Wisdom and knowledge are my brothers
mysteries of the universe lie at my feet
I am one with the sun, the stars, the earth,
and all living organisms that embrace life
I am one with mother-life and father-death
I am one with the natural forces that binds body
and soul to the ultimate laws of creation
I am one
I am one
I am one with God

A Question

Heavenly winds are shrieking
across a dark and sinister sky
The eternal knight is coming
with his avenging shaft of light
Demonic forces of darkness
forming rank in the unholy night
The very gates of hell are shaking
who can stand against this might?
The heavenly hosts are gathering
vowing to vanquish or to die
The great battle of life has unfolded
this old earth has paid a heavy price
The vast forces of darkness are broken
we all gather those few who survived
The brilliance of glory stood before us
as we staggered towards its light
As we crossed the last bridge to heaven
a question God put to each and every child
When you seek the road to salvation
can you walk the very last mile?

Where

Where is little Billy Jack,
who loved to play in the sand?
His mother would always wash his face,
then she would hold his little hand.

Where is little Billy Jack,
with boyish tears sparkling in his eyes?
They took him away to boot camp;
they told him not to cry.

Where is little Billy Jack,
whom they taught to be a man?
They took away his humanity;
the army told him he was grand.

Where is little Billy Jack,
does he now rest quietly in a field?
They flew him to Southeast Asia
they taught him how to kill.

Where is little Billy Jack?
his small head buried halfway in the sand
There is nobody there to wash his face;
now only God holds his little hand.

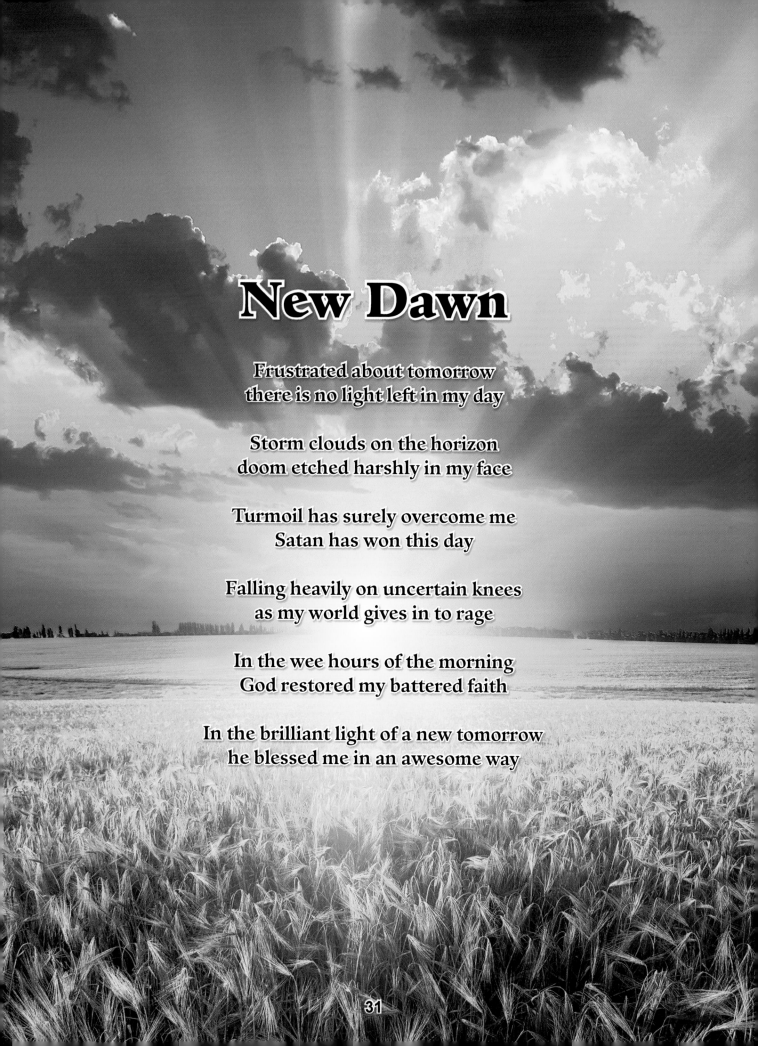

New Dawn

Frustrated about tomorrow
there is no light left in my day

Storm clouds on the horizon
doom etched harshly in my face

Turmoil has surely overcome me
Satan has won this day

Falling heavily on uncertain knees
as my world gives in to rage

In the wee hours of the morning
God restored my battered faith

In the brilliant light of a new tomorrow
he blessed me in an awesome way

Once I Had a Valentine

Once I had a valentine
a foolish love that has just washed ashore
winds of desire have come and gone
passion has stopped its roar

Once I had a valentine
who vowed to love me forever more
somehow in the confusing complexity of life
love forever shouted nevermore

Once I had a valentine
within my arms, she refused to soar
with tears of sadness and a reluctant key
my wounded heart unlocked the door

Once I had a valentine
a lovely spirit not meant for me
I adore her still, and I always will
with love, I set her free

Once I had a valentine

Companion

Close down your mind
shut out the night

Bow your head
let God inside

Bare open your soul
let in his light

Feel his glow
let his healing flow

When life goes wrong
he will keep you strong

Just open up your heart
God will do his part

Never walk alone
take God along

Loving You

Will you not let me hold you, love you—adore you
my hands want only to explore you
yet curiously, my sensuality seems only to be abhorrent

My fervent wish is simply to be near you
to revere you—to know you
to quietly bask in the passionate glow of your esteem

I desperately need to mate you, to taste you, to sate you
to placate this deep yearning of want
that I have harbored, all through our troubled years

I dare to kiss you—to miss you, to scold you, to hold you
to walk heart to true heart
into the awesome odyssey of love's embrace

For, dear heart, to know you is to love you
and to love you is to desire you
and that desire is etched upon the shackles of my heart

I love you

Just Try

What does it matter if you're behind in the race
your lungs are bursting; you fall flat on your face
just try

Don't listen when others complain
you must pay your price and ignore your pain
just try

Too tired and exhausted to remember your name
you have given your all—don't be ashamed
just try

Have courage when you run the race
when the hills seems high; the wind in your face
just try

You choke on your fear, don't bury your pride
you really have nothing to lose if you try
just try

Let determination infuse your core
faith is your wings; get ready to soar
just try

The Fight

When the magical moments are gone
your beleaguered heart feels encased in stone

When you are feeling so much alone
no arms there to comfort you or to keep you strong

Feeling so hurt that you'll never really forgive
words so harshly spoken, it might take many years

Closed minds no longer willing to share
precious moments abandoned in utter despair

The music of love left behind in erratic flight
no bodies touching in the tenderness of night

In matters of the heart, there is no wrong or right
no way to take it back when lovers have a fight

Flowers

Flowers
dancing gently in the breeze.

Flowers
smiling brightly through their leaves.

Flowers
growing contentedly at your feet.

Flowers
filling the air so sweet.

Flowers
gathering by the creek.

Lovely flowers
a natural sign of peace.

Nothing
dwarfs the beauty of a flower, not even the sea.

Dear God
are there lovelier things than these?

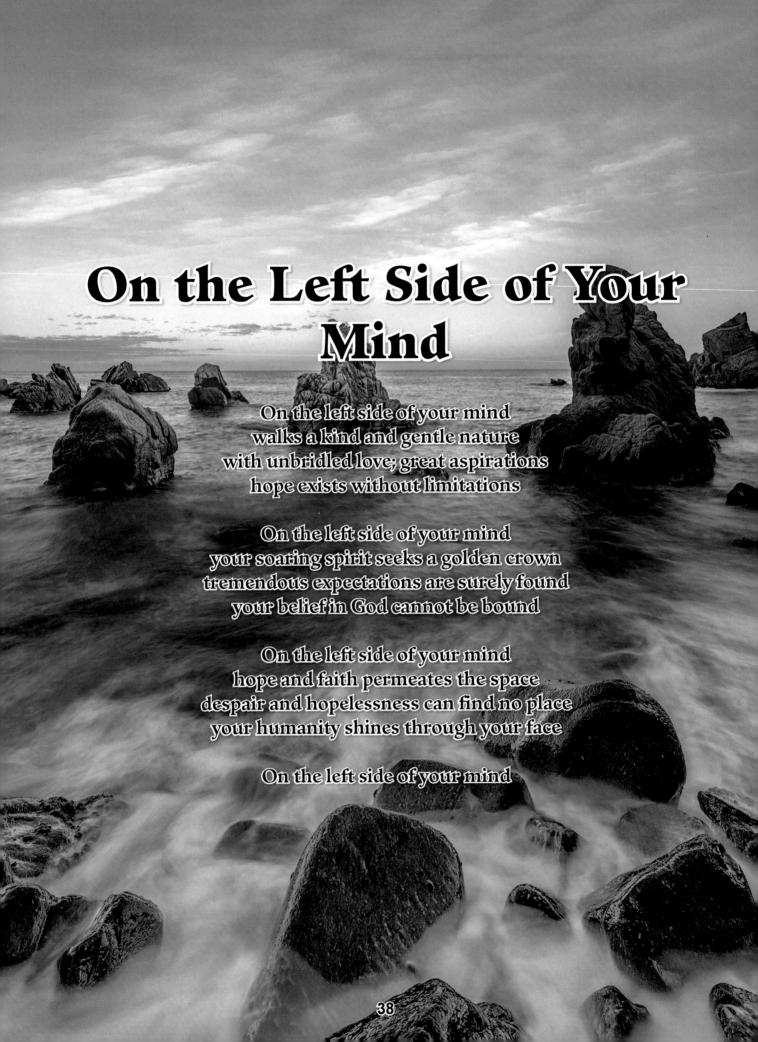

On the Left Side of Your Mind

On the left side of your mind
walks a kind and gentle nature
with unbridled love; great aspirations
hope exists without limitations

On the left side of your mind
your soaring spirit seeks a golden crown
tremendous expectations are surely found
your belief in God cannot be bound

On the left side of your mind
hope and faith permeates the space
despair and hopelessness can find no place
your humanity shines through your face

On the left side of your mind

Beyond Slavery

We, once the scattered children of God's creation
without a birthright, without a nation

Beaten, suppressed beyond all civilized imagination
born without hope, without representation

With bloodstained backs, King Cotton in our sacks
our great African heritage somehow remained intact

Even in this time of conflict, out beyond the strife
we saw a new tomorrow beyond the 'southern lights'

You see, the cycle of life has come once again
the cycle of unity, the circle of friends

So no more tears of sadness nor tears of sorrow
we celebrate our greatest harvest

Ourselves

With Love

A wife is not a perfected dream
with awe-inspiring qualities of mind and body it seems
Neither is she a star-studded queen
living in a fantasy-land of magical dragons and things
A wife is the sweet, sweet joy of life
add, a touch of sugar, a dab of honey, and a pinch of spice
This lovely lady shares your bed at night
tucking cold loving feet against the warmth of your back
She is the great love of your life
she is your heart's desire, your fire and ice, that's a fact
My wife like all wives can do no wrong
she is proud, she is beautiful, she is remarkably strong
My wife could be the title of a song ; the title being
"With Such A Love, How Can I Go Wrong"

Enough Said

The sky is falling
and all isn't well
may I suggest to you
to run like hell!

Ole Friend

Don't know why I miss you so
You seem to be always on my mind
Why do I stare at faces in a crowd?
Guess I expect to see your silly smile

Don't know where time has come and gone
Don't know why this moment feels so wrong
I only know that you won't be coming home
Since you left me, I feel so much alone

So each night as I kneel to pray
I asked the good lord to make a way
For ole friends to meet again face-to-face
To fondly embrace at heaven's gate

Inner Gold

Look into my mind's eye
and try to discover the inner me;
A faceless soul guarding a battered door,
tightly grasping a tarnished key
Place your ear against the floor,
and you will hear my lifeblood roar.
For you have entered a sacred place
where my reality confronts its source.
If you would look beyond the door
you'll discover a lovely world
A place where time has come to rest,
a place where dreams unfurl.
Passions like silver streaks of lightning
they rage gloriously across my sky.
You can see them clearly from the outside
if you would look deep within my eyes
My world is sadness, my world is joy
my exquisite world of endless dreams
A world of love, a world of peace,
a world where compassion reigns.
I went searching through my inner mind
curious to see what I would find
In my mind, a bold treasure I've found
a rare beauty that is all mine.

Distant Shores

I cannot touch you with my mind
to share a love you're reluctant to find

I cannot restore the many lost years
that unrelenting fate has stripped away

I cannot restore the uncertain familiarity
that the passage of time has delayed

I can only ride the tides of my life
on a distant shore, I endured toil and strife

My heart is sad on this very special day
when at last, son, we come face-to-face

Please, do not hate me son; I do pray
our paths have veered in separate ways

My love for you has grown stronger
with each passing day.

Where Has America Gone?

Lord, our black preachers, did they sell us out?
our social conscience is riddled with doubt
Another Trayvon Martin was just stricken down
I guess anything goes when you lie helpless on the ground
Black men used as cannon fodder in a white man's senseless war
but he is just another nigger in a redneck bar
Where has America gone?

Walked hand in hand with the chief of police
we sought justice; we sought peace
Now where are those who were in favor?
those who applauded our nonviolent behavior
The court still plays us for fools
black folks are guilty as a general rule
Where has America gone?

Welfare, food stamps, "Boy! Keep your black ass in line"
Drug dealers, crackheads, all are running out of time
Gangbanging, clan hangings, Nazism on the rise
black boys dying, "Dey moma's crying," education in decline
Black communities running out of hope
guess what, there is plenty of dope
Where has America gone?

Lack of motivation, low expectations, suicide rules desperate lives
ghetto killing fields, carjacking thrills, a nation where intolerance thrives
Where in hell is the dream? Did it die with Martin Luther King?
"Preacher—don't feed me any mo' pie in the sky!"
The time is at hand to stand up and be a man
because it looks like genocide
Where has America gone?

The Gale

Walk with me; I blow conscience free
but let the average man beware
My tale is old; I possess no soul
my abode is water, wind, and air
Holding your ground? I'll knock you down!
bask fearfully in the power that's mine
Washed many to sea; screaming as they flee
my immense power assuredly abounds
I shun the light; I crave the night
my howling roar foretells your pain
Mariners called me evil; many call me foul
mindless destruction comes with my rains
I lurk at sea, where misfortune sleeps
come and try your fate in my winds
I carry no joy; I carry no hope
only sorrow rides the crest of my waves
I'll take your life and widow your wife
I'll suspend you in a watery grave
I blow near and far, doom in the dark
I wait relentlessly in the darkest night
I sense the false hope; I got you by the throat
I sense the mortal fear you harbor inside
Why cast stormy emotions at another?
Can't find the calm seas inside you brother?
Just like my savage winds, blowing here; there;
with total indifference, without care
You'll truly call no man a friend

Quiet

A single motionless teardrop
in a worried father's eye

The wordless emotional feeling
a young soldier gathers up his pride

The unnatural silence
before the military plane arrives

The empty heartfelt moment
after a son has said good-bye

The horror-struck stillness
as the roar of battle fades away

The calm desperation
on a dying young soldier's face

The empty, tranquil instant
when death has sealed his fate

A young widow's muffled grieving
a tearful father kneels quietly to pray

Sunshine for Hannah

Where does the sun go
after it wanders across the sky
warming your face with hope and grace
and illuminating your Swedish eyes?
Where does the sun go
after conceiving a fresh new day?
Does it really fall into the shimmering sea
and then sparkle beneath the waves?
Where does your sun go, Hannah
after traversing its endless miles?
I can hear it in your laughter
I see the brilliance when you smile

Dreams

My dreaming days are over, my son;
my dreams are at an end.

My dreams will never die, my son,
because in you, I will dream again.

So dream all the dreams you can, my son,
for in life, dreams transcend the sky.

Dreams pierce the eternal night, my son,
and reality reaps its light.

I see you don't comprehend my mind, my son,
but when it's your time to die,

You will see a future you were not meant to see
reflected in your son's eyes.

I dreamed of you before you were born;
now that dream sits here at my feet.

Son, your life did not begin in your mother's womb;
your life began in my dream.

From You to Me

A little bird came by today
with a message on his wing

It spoke of love and gentle things
and of your loving ways it sang

Of peace, joy, and happy thoughts
my heart did flutter and bang

Of flowers, candy, and sweeter things
his little voice did ring

But best of all, of all his gifts
was the beauty of your name

He said it twice, so soft, so nice
like a gentle breath of spring

Heaven

I see a place that occupies no space
calm winds blow across a shimmering sea

A place of emerald-green forest
beautiful, winged creatures abide in peace

As I gaze across this glorious land
upon a golden hilltop, I saw a man

He looked clean through my eternal soul
he then stretches out his loving hands

I am in this place that occupies no space
where amber leaves fall from a brilliant sky

In this glorious land, I've made my stand
this perfect man walks by my side

Dewdrops

Dewdrops glittering in the morning sun
like countless drops of pearls

Creating such a beautiful site, it's as though
you're in a crystal world

Dewdrops gathering on roses so red
sheer radiance compels the naked eye

Leaving behind such a wondrous effect
its beauty makes you want to cry

Dewdrops shimmering in a cold blue sky
how it makes the air so sweet

Dewdrops collecting on my father's grave
Lord, forgive him; let him rest in peace

True Love

You don't have to love me
as much as I truly love you.
My love is so unbelievably strong;
I'll just pretend you do.

You don't have to want me
as much as I really want you.
My wants are so unselfish;
my wants are enough for two.

You don't have to hold me
as much as I desire to hold you.
I'll just embrace you with my eyes,
there's no need to bother you.

You don't have to need me
as much as I surely need you.
Please don't overly concern yourself;
all my needs are fulfilled in you.

You don't have to believe in me
as much as I believe in you.
My faith in you is so unerringly;
because my love is true.

Reflections

You know God only put us here for just a little while
to glorify his name, share his perfect love with our less-than-perfect lives

Can't see where this long road ends as I struggle from day-to-day
along the way, so many mistakes, why God still loves me I cannot say

Even contemplating this walk to glory, never realized it would be so hard
the rivers are too wide, valleys too deep; sheer mountains dearly tax my heart

But as I walk along this road of life, there is one truth I must duly note
if you look beyond the light of God's love, it's where the darkest shadows grow

Life can sometimes be most ironic; it will spiral right out of your control
when confusion and fear surrounds you; counter with faith and hope

So take a critical look at your life; cherish the precious time you have
remember, the ultimate prize of life awaits you; rejoice don't despair

Even when you are at your worst, bowing down on bended knees
God has never locked the door of life—his saving grace is the only key

So never ever regret your life, even if you stray from the path
God will never forsake you; his undying love will lead you back

What If

What if I could speak with the voice of an angel
could recite every tongue known to men?

What if I knew everything that will ever happen
could reveal your future and how it would end?

What if my faith could move the mighty mountains
and I would dare to look into the heart of the sun?

What if I could walk upon the sweltering ocean
calm the troubled waters by raising my arms?

What if I could cross the world's harshest desert
and slay a mighty dragon with a word on my tongue?

What if I could raise the dead from their slumber
and breathe back life into eviscerated lungs?

What if I could control both thunder and lightning
could shake the whole world by striking the ground?

What if I could wave away all poverty and sickness
bringing about peace where it's never been found?

What if I could abolish all needless warfare
and gift to the whole world a long-lasting peace?

What if I could create everything I would imagine
with the reality being a virtual part of me?

What if God's word is all I could ask for
What if his love is all that I need?

What if ....

The Thought of You

For just one of your precious smiles
You realize I'd walk a thousand miles

For just one glance into your secret heart
I would literally pull this world apart

How your eyes pierce my very soul
What tremendous power you hold

Can't stand to watch you sob and weep
Use my tears to abate your grief

If anything in this life causes you pain
I will bear your hurt; I won't complain

Just to give you a moment of perfect peace
My own contentment soars beyond belief

When you so quietly whisper my name
My world is never quite the same

Hope to never say a last good-bye
My manly tears would rend the sky

Everything in this life that I do
Reminds me how much I love you

Black Boy

Black boy, black boy, know not from whence you came
your point of origin or your christian name

Let no one tell you how far you should go
wherever it leads, only the good Lord really knows

Never embrace mediocrity, trying to be like everyone else
take pride in your accomplishments; take pride in yourself

For at the crest of the hill is where your challenge lies
victory is not cheap, but the rewards are high

I see the gleam in your eyes, your confident stride
black skin can't hide the tremendous potential inside

Black boy, black boy, don't ever hold your head in shame
we paid your price of freedom with our suffering and pain

Down the road of life when you become 'all the rage'
please try to remember how your road was paved

A Tribute

Crying quietly into your pillow
after your hungry kids are put to rest,
your nights are filled with turmoil
for your tomorrows are full of dread.

Your husband just up and left you—
his commitment ended at your bed;
you're left with many little mouths to feed,
you pray,"Dear Jesus, they must be fed."

So you cry softly into your pillow,
trying to quell your inner doubts;
there is no food in your pantry—
money is scarce when you're down and out.

But somehow you find the energy
to keep going and scratching along;
you hug your kids, look into their eyes,
you realize that you must stay strong

Sometimes you're less than victorious,
your spirit is downtrodden and weak,
you're blessed with such an intensive faith
you will never admit defeat.

For the race of life goes not to the swift
but to those who would struggle on.
suppressing fear in the depths of your mind,
you protected your fragile home.

You've been a lost child of destiny
you have taught your children well.
Cried enough tears to fill the deep blue sea
but your courage rode high in the swells

I pay tribute to you, mother, you and all others
whose tireless endeavors have passed life's test.
May God make you a place in his eternal land;
don't cry, Mom—he knows you did your best.

The Source

Close down your mind
shut out the night

Bow your troubled head
invite God inside

Bare open your darkened soul
bask in his light

Feel his powerful glow
let his healing flow

Let him ease your pain
he will bear the strain

Let him heal your heart
he'll do his part

When life goes wrong
he will keep you strong

In your bleakest hour
he is your source of power

A Note from Heaven

The book of life was opened and then closed
God called my name; it was my time to go

The pure irony of life is that death is a key
To open up doors we are reluctant to see

Did you really believe all my hope was gone?
Don't hang your head; my father called me home

My true spirit still lives in your secret heart
This notion of death cannot pull us apart

My precious love will continue to shine
In mournful eyes, in the recesses of your minds

Surely, you know that God still talks to me
Just in a quieter voice on a whispering breeze

So children, enjoy your life and live it free
My mind is at rest; my soul is at peace . . .

Mom

My World

In my eyes, I see a world of unbridled glory
Possibilities exist at every turn

Doubt can sustain no meaningful, solid purchase
The spirit of lack doesn't know my name

Somebody, please destroy the word impossible
Try living life without guilt or shame

My world consists of many amazing miracles
Where there's no fault, there's no one to blame

An unselfish heart has been my only mentor
An untroubled mind doesn't cause me pain

Why not try this life of perfect peace and wonder?
Your unguarded soul will never be the same

I can't conceive of this awful term we call surrender
Victory, the only word I'll ever claim

In this grand life, it never pays to be a pretender
Lack of faith can make you go insane

When you are no longer a worthy, top contender
Have courage to right an obvious wrong

Why not live in a world of rare beauty and splendor?
Do place your faith upon a living throne

My Hero

My hero is a little boy
whose innocence has touched my soul.

My hero is a little boy
whose smile fate has turned to gold.

My hero is a little boy
whose hand has reached out to mine.

My hero is a little boy
whose love breached the barriers of my mind.

My hero is a little boy
whose age is only three.

My hero is a little boy
who to my heart has found the key.

Lonely

Made myself a promise today to feel real grand, let life have its way
I even laughed; I danced, and I tried to smile my blues away
My true feelings were hidden behind all the merriment I made

My mind raved, how do I make it through another tedious day?
Maybe I'll write, recite, or tell spiffy jokes all night
Possibly read a new book to gain a new and dramatic insight

Why, I could twiddle my thumbs—that could be tremendous fun
What about playing some funky music or writing exhilarating puns?
There are astronomical things to do to provide a measure of fun or two

I could drown my sorrows in a large bucket of Kentucky Fried
Or pass out on a grand ole bottle of whiskey and rye
Look at the significant time this bold venture would occupy

But, dearest heart, my true feelings clearly I cannot hide
It's very difficult to keep my heartache and loneliness inside
Give me credit, I try--maybe I just need a good cry

Double Trouble

Lord, where does real trouble begin
With little angels so ripe with sin?

Hide your breakables; I will say no more
Pull down your curtains and lock the friggin' door

The cute little monsters are on the prowl
Don't be fooled by the laughter and glorious smiles

These little ruffians will steal your peace
Capture your heart, then dance on your feet

Grandpaw was the poor "horsey" who came up lame
They rode him past exhaustion—they had no shame

I asked God to help me as I lay upon the floor
I was soundly chastised—I was asked to do more

Why me, Lord? I never signed up for this
There is a wet spot on my back; it smells like piss

I warned dear Grandmaw not to open the door
"Just tell them, bad kids, we don't live here anymore"

Too bad this tactic doesn't work like a charm
It's a wonder how wet kisses can work to disarm

To all future Grandpaws, if you ever have twins
Run like hell because there's no way you'll win

There's a load in that one diaper that's suspiciously thick
Oh god, it's awful; it smells like shi——

Gangbanger

Yo, you should come and join my gang, bro; let me show you how we bang
See that old 'dummy,' we take his money; we beat him with his 'friggin' cane

I'm a real bad-ass boy; got lots of scars; I do the 'drive-byes' for the gang
Guns are my toys, a knife is my joy; some people say I'm insane

I'm gonna help you make your name ,bro; I just love to bring on the pain
Burned down my moma's house; killed her puppy with a rusty chain

I destroy peoples hope; I sell em dope, see that crackhead walking in the rain
Yo! Better have my money tonight, I'm gonna blow out yo pea-sized brain

I'm the baddest brother in this pack, you gotta be impressed with that
I really need you to join this gang, bro; somebody needs to watch my back

You feel me, bro?

Life Again

I can feel the stillness on this eerie night
I bind no fear, no sorrow, no strife

My tormented soul is free to seek its rest
I fought a great battle; I gave it my best

A body tires from all the suffering within
My spirit feels defeated; does my destiny end ?

The battle of life can no longer be contained
My stark reality is consumed with pain

My wounds have blinded me; I could not see
This passion for life burns so formidable in me

Heavenly Light

There's light at the end of this tunnel
It has helped me to find my way
I found hope at the end of this tunnel
That bright hope shines upon my face
There is love at the end of this tunnel
My spirit basked in its glorious rays
That lone light at the end of my tunnel
It calls to my salvation, my joy, my faith
That same light is at the end of your tunnel
Please make sure it doesn't fade away

Little Bad Boy's Prayer

God, ya lit my doggy die; Mom says it's 'cause I'm so bad
She says ya took 'im away from me 'cause I made ya mad
If you bring 'im back ta me, I'll try 'xtra hard ta be good
Take my bafth, comb my 'air—yuck--do like mom says I should
My doggie meant a lot ta me—he was dah only little friend I had
Hold up, God, gotta take a quick pee; my baby bruther
Mom's little angel just walked under this tree
Got 'im!!

Just Say I Do

I see a vision of loveliness
Beauty surrounds her like a breath of light
Soft brown eyes give meaning to glorious
Sunlight pales before a brilliant smile

Have I not loved her beyond this lifetime?
Seems that I have waited for her all of my life
I dreamed of her beyond the scarlet sunset
I danced with her in the morning sky

Let me adore her beyond all tomorrows
My poor heart will most likely expire
Just one look, and the world I would surrender
One kiss, how does a sane man survive?

Please forgive me for my impertinence
I have desired you for a very long time
Am I wrong to imagine that you love me?
A less foolish man would protect his pride

Don't know how I've come to love you
But without your regard, I would most likely die
I would defy the vast forces of eternity
I'd move heaven and earth to make you my wife

Just Me

I've hands to feel, eyes to see, and a mind to know
A generous heart with selfless love that overflows
I am only a man, not God; I am only just a man
I've been shamed, blamed, conspired in many things
Most often, I think I'm right, more often not so bright
People have different definitions of wrong and right
Intelligence is not a basic criteria to know all things
Old-fashion common sense is much better than brains
We are all inconsistent in our knowledge of life
In short, we all make mistakes even with great insight
Life goes on when conditions seem just wrong
I live, and I breathe, no doubt, I will eventually die
I've made the best of my life, and when I go on
my family will bring flowers, make speeches and cry
You do know, a man is not a bird, a place, or a tree
Neither is he a being of what's called perfect harmony
Man is the sole creator of his own illusive destiny
God does give him a choice in a quiet, infinite voice
I only know what I know that feels real to me
To this end and only this end, I strive to set my soul free
When all is said and done, can't you see
I can only be just me.

To Life

Funny how unpredictable life can be
as we travel this salvation road
We do our best, pray away the rest
as we hope to cleanse our souls
Walking along this great road of life
most often, we will find despair
Yet the sun still shines, rain still falls
when our circumstances seem unfair
God will do what only God can do
make a wise choice and take his hand
He will abate your tears, calm your fears,
taking your soul to a promised land
The fullness of life is all the time you have
not the length nor the span of years
The completion of life, your task at hand,
you must conquer and manage your fears
The cycle of life is not the end of life,
it is the beginning of something new
So find your lost faith, state your case,
rest assured that God will honor you

Trucking with Love

Truck, truck, which way do you go
maybe to Ohio on this busy road?
Truck, truck, you carry such a heavy load
maybe another passenger you could hold?
Truck, truck, I really should let you know
my heart's desire lives at the end of your road
Truck, truck, I know you must go on
please take my heart along

Forever God

In the quiet stillness of an early morn
I hear the sweet, sweet echoes of an angel's horn

Why me, Lord? What do you seek?
I am just another lost soul, driven beyond your reach

Yet you reach down to soothe my mortal pain
Yet you look down, and you forgive my tremendous shame

Just let me die, Lord, for you know that I am no good
Remove your hand, Lord, and let me perish as I should

Still you cast your light, Lord, when darkness is at my back
Why do you stay the night, Lord, when my soul is under attack?

Why do you love me, Lord, when I do not love myself?
Why would you forgive me, Lord, when the only road I seek is hell?

Yet you reach down, Lord, to ease my wounded soul
Why do you continue to strive, Lord, to make the imperfect whole?

But you stayed, Lord, when I was cast into the thorns
I felt your grace, Lord, when you cradled me within your arms

You heard my prayer, Lord, when everyone turned their backs
You dared to touch me when my immortal soul was tainted black

Forgive me, Lord, for all the wrong that I have done
Forgive me, Lord, because of you, I am coming home

So in the quiet stillness of an early morn
I can hear the sweet, sweet echoes of an angel's horn

The Storm

There is a strange storm coming across this barren, broken land
I can hear the roar of thunder; best beware, you foolish man
The evil forces of darkness will now be washed away by truth
The awesome winds of hatred will no longer plague or trouble you
Keep your eyes upon the heavens for his mighty glory is at hand
Blessed are the truly faithful; it takes courage to rise, to stand
The slayer of the ungodly is before us, golden shaft in the morning sky
The righteous need not cover—the wrath of heaven will pass them by
My voice shouted out the victory and the coming of the Lord
The storm of life will not ignore us; let's change our sinful hearts

Yes, It's You

You must believe it if you ever want to receive it
with great expectations you'll always be blessed
Don't entertain false hope—it's really a knotted rope
don't kill your golden goose, just finish your quest
Know in your heart that you can surely achieve it
your absolute belief is your real key to success
So please don't ever look back at what you lack
your radical faith will quickly fill in the rest
Life will scrape some hide, don't lose your pride
fulfill your promise, there will be no regrets

The Flight

Let me rise above the mountains
my spirit seeks a higher means of flight
How far can the stars be above the heavens
my sacred wish to fly beyond this sky
My soul has floundered beneath redemption
my will seeks to surpass the speed of light
The wind cannot touch my exalted ego,
the mighty sun is simply too weak to try
Dare I fly into the mighty realm of heaven
beyond eternity, beyond the ever night
There is no darkness, there is no shadow
there's only brilliance ,there is only this light
My spirit has entered this place of wonder
beyond imagination is the kingdom of life
My soul has completed its amazing journey
my soul has completed its flight

Edwards Brothers Malloy
Ann Arbor MI. USA
April 28, 2017